STYLE ICONS

Marilyn Monroe

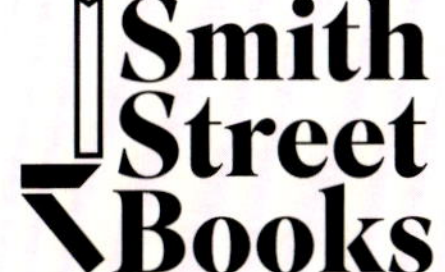

KELLY SMITH & ELIZABETH WEITZMAN

Blonde Ambition

MARILYN MONROE: STYLE, STARDOM, AND SELF-INVENTION

When we think of Marilyn Monroe today, it's as an ineffably glamorous fashion icon. Consider her white halter dress in *The Seven Year Itch*, fluttering up in such daring fashion. Her breathtaking pink satin column gown in *Gentlemen Prefer Blondes*, sparkling with custom-designed jewels. Or, of course, the shimmering, nude-illusion gown she wore to President Kennedy's 45th birthday celebration, for the sexiest serenade in history.

She also developed a unique walk to take full advantage of her hourglass figure, and designed hair and makeup palettes that allowed her to appear lit from within.

But even she acknowledged that playing "Marilyn Monroe" – the superstar with an impossibly dazzling presence – was the greatest, and most challenging, performance of her life.

It's common knowledge that Monroe started life as Norma Jeane Mortenson, but not many people realize just how far she had to climb to get there. She was born into poverty in 1926, and spent her childhood shuffling between disinterested relatives, an orphanage, and foster homes around the outskirts of Los Angeles.

In 1944, 18-year-old Norma Jeane was working in an aircraft factory when a photographer asked to take her picture. Shortly afterward, she left her job and her husband of two years to reinvent herself as a pin-up model and aspiring actor. She was determined to shape her own destiny, and within a few years, she was appearing in leading film roles. But that early success also marked the start of industry efforts to undermine her.

Marilyn Monroe, as she was now known, was swiftly typecast as a ditzy blonde. Although she was happy to play that role on film, she resented being treated as such offscreen. In reality, she was a driven, self-made woman who founded her own production company, became an outspoken supporter of the civil rights movement, and studied her craft at the esteemed Actors Studio in New York.

She was also a naturally gifted performer. She's a comic delight as savvy seductress Lorelei Lee in *Gentlemen Prefer Blondes*, brings an unexpected sweetness to the ultimate male fantasy in *The Seven Year Itch*, and is genuinely heartbreaking as a gentle cowgirl in *The Misfits*.

We can see, as we look back at her career, how many attempts she made to show us who she really was. This is especially clear in her personal style, which remained determinedly casual whenever she was able to evade the responsibilities of her overwhelming fame.

Sadly, Monroe lived in a time when women could be defined by intelligence or appearance, but not both. She was repeatedly let down by the knowledge that everyone wanted to look, but no one wanted to see. Even today, her vulnerability can break your heart. As Lorelei says in *Gentlemen Prefer Blondes*, "It's a terrible thing to be lonesome. Especially in the middle of a crowd."

Hollywood has given us plenty of sought-after sex symbols, but it was Monroe who became the ultimate icon. Her legacy is defined not only by her appearance, but her inner self. In films and photo shoots, her intelligence, humor, and humanity are as clearly evident as her breathtaking beauty.

INSTRUCTIONS

To use, carefully press out the doll and cross-piece and assemble the stand as shown below.

Use scissors to snip the cross-piece and stand.

Slot the cross-piece into the flaps and fold the tabs to secure it.

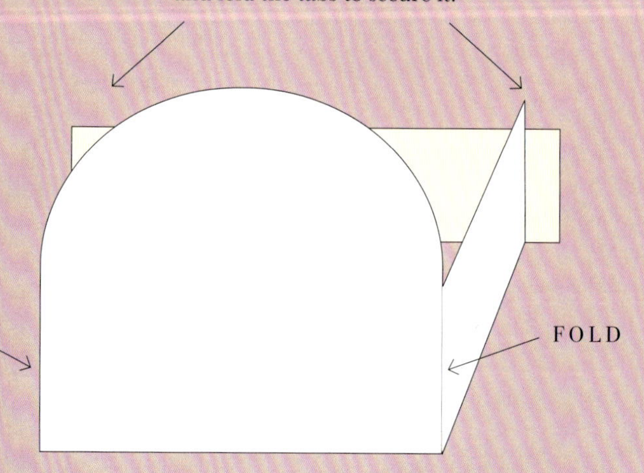

Press out the outfits and get dressing.
Style Marilyn in her iconic looks, or mix and match
to create something brand new.

LIFE MAGAZINE FEATURE

At Home in Hollywood

PHOTOGRAPHED BY ALFRED EISENSTAEDT

By early 1953, Monroe had appeared in several movies, including the Oscar-winning *All About Eve*. But she was still known, in the words of gossip columnist Hedda Hopper, as a "cheesecake queen." Nude pictures of her taken years earlier had just resurfaced, and her public profile was dominated by a tumultuous relationship with baseball legend Joe DiMaggio. But she also had a driving ambition and was ready to build a serious and lasting career.

It's no accident that the spread for *LIFE* magazine, shot when she was just 26, was so stripped down – and that she wasn't. For this session, she made sure that the acclaimed photographer, Alfred Eisenstaedt, captured her reading, writing, and relaxed – the very qualities Hollywood so often ignored. Monroe spent much of her life determined to demonstrate her depth, both personally and professionally, and these photographs are symbolic of her strength and wisdom. For his part, Eisenstaedt treated her with gentle respect and she looks strikingly comfortable in her own skin as a result.

We can already see the blonde bob and winged eyeliner that she'd make famous, but it's noteworthy that both her tousled hair and youthful makeup are far more relaxed than you'd expect for a major magazine shoot. Her casual outfits, which she chose herself, are equally telling: a plain black turtleneck paired with slim, mid-rise white and gingham capris are the very definition of barefoot breeziness.

Though Monroe would later adopt an overtly glamorous image, she rarely radiated more confidence – or a more luminous beauty – than she did under Eisenstaedt's nonjudgmental lens.

1953

GENTLEMEN PREFER BLONDES

Opening Scene

DIRECTED BY HOWARD HAWKS

Monroe knew that her body was her calling card – not her only gift, just the one that got her in the door. She was used to being undervalued, and worked hard to dispel people's assumptions about her. So, too, did her finest costume designer, William "Billy" Travilla. Travilla outfitted her for eight films, and their collaborations were shaped by mutual trust. When he said his designs for Monroe were "an act of love," he meant it.

Howard Hawks' delightful musical comedy opens with a wink and a song: "We're just two little girls from Little Rock," coo Monroe and her co-star Jane Russell. But Travilla's slinky, red-sequined gowns make it quite clear that they're neither little girls nor shrinking violets. These sophisticated ladies, shimmering in dresses cut up to here and down to there, know exactly what they're doing – hunting for husbands. It's interesting to note that Travilla – a craftsman as well as an artist – included a scattering of beige sequins hidden within his scarlet design. Onscreen, Monroe gravitated toward clothes with sparkle, and Travilla knew this small but essential detail would go a long way toward adding some extra shine.

Gentlemen Prefer Blondes was based on a bestselling novel by Anita Loos, who was inspired by the much-married Ziegfeld Girl and self-proclaimed "gold digger" Peggy Hopkins Joyce. A full collection of jewels, enhanced by a matching feathered headpiece and peep-toe heels, announces Marilyn's Lorelei Lee as a force to be reckoned with. Diamanté wrist-wraps and cuffs, ruby-drop earrings offset by a massive matching necklace, and a palm-sized brooch sitting pretty on her hip? It's a great start, sure, but for this girl, there's always room for more.

Wide-eyed Lorelei is both adorable and astute: As men fall for her pneumatic charms, she sizes them up and begins her own seductions. But, in characteristic Monroe fashion, she does it with so much appeal that we're on her side from the start, and we stay there to the end.

1953

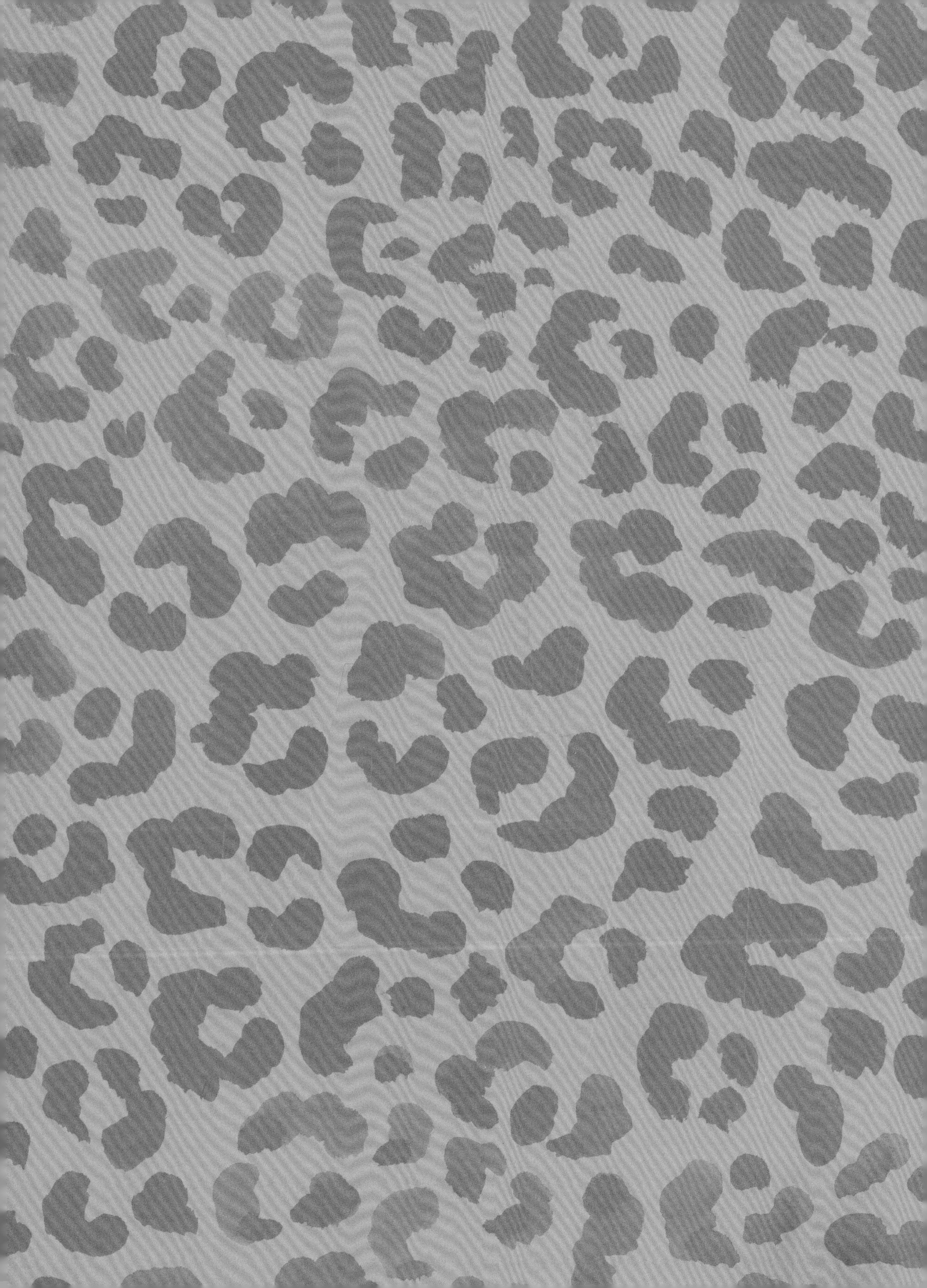

GENTLEMEN PREFER BLONDES

Traveling to France

DIRECTED BY HOWARD HAWKS

"Pardon me, is this the way to Europe, France?" Lorelei asks as she glides toward an ocean liner bound for Cherbourg. But she's turned the gangplank into a catwalk, so nobody's listening – they're too busy looking.

Costume designer Billy Travilla was a master of balance, so Lorelei's navy traveling outfit covers all, while still being cut close enough to show off every curve. Her pillbox hat, proper pumps, and nude gloves intimate a ladylike demurity. But her matching leopard muff and split cape neckline, paired with gold and diamond jewelry at each available pulse point (not to mention those platinum curls and that strong red lip) suggest luxury with just a hint of wildness – exactly what Lorelei is offering to the highest bidder.

As an actor, Monroe was never looser or more lovely than in *Gentlemen Prefer Blondes*. It was her first true blockbuster – the film that transformed her from starlet to celestial force. Her timing is impeccable, and she's working on multiple levels as the sweetest gold digger there ever was. She sashays through every scene in Travilla's gloriously form-fitting costumes while sending up her own sexpot persona with joyful wit, making sure we're all in on the joke.

Her performance is so deft that we never doubt Lorelei's ability to snag a "suitable gentleman" – which is to say, one who can keep her covered in … well, just wait a few pages.

1953

GENTLEMEN PREFER BLONDES

Diamonds Are a Girl's Best Friend

DIRECTED BY HOWARD HAWKS

There is no more iconic Monroe ensemble than this strapless pink dress laden with diamond accessories. But the legendary look from this memorable musical number almost didn't happen.

Billy Travilla's original design – a risqué showgirl costume made of little more than fishnets and some strategically placed gems – was nixed at the last minute by the studio. So he swerved. Instead of creating a nearly nude spectacle, he transformed Lorelei into the embodiment of luxe elegance. She is instantly unforgettable in this shocking-pink silk-satin gown, lined in black and accentuated with a theatrical bustle bow and matching opera gloves. After observing the scene's complex choreography, Travilla transformed his planned two-piece ensemble into a single, strapless column. Then he added a sexy slit in the back, to make it easier for Monroe to move.

This glittering vision is further enhanced by a dramatic diamanté choker, as well as sparkly earrings and stunning wrist cuffs, all designed by renowned jewelers Joseff of Hollywood.

In 1985, Madonna threw a new spotlight on the sequence when she recrafted it for her "Material Girl" music video. Madonna's version is intentionally edgy – all appetite and avarice. By contrast, Monroe's gentle humor reads like a revelation today: she's less a material girl than a sensible one.

Like Lorelei, Monroe lived in an era when professional women were viewed with suspicion and bound by a thicket of double standards. There weren't many ways for a lady to earn a living in 1953, which is why her characters often approached marriage as a vocation. Lorelei's logic is purely practical: If men choose wives in part for their appearance, is it really so unreasonable for the wives to have a few requirements as well?

1953

The Seven Year Itch

DIRECTED BY BILLY WILDER

By 1955, Monroe was the world's most recognizable sex symbol, and this Billy Wilder comedy was structured entirely around male fantasy. Tom Ewell plays Richard Sherman, a middle-aged dad who falls for his beautiful young neighbor during a steamy summer when his wife has escaped to the beach and he's stuck alone in the city. The script didn't give Monroe's character much dimension – she's credited only as "The Girl" – so it was up to her to develop more depth. And that's exactly what she did, turning The Girl into an amusingly earnest sweetheart who reminds Richard that, deep down, he truly does love his wife.

But none of that really matters, because this movie is now remembered for a single moment: Monroe standing in strappy white stilettos over an NYC subway grate, cooling herself off as the pleated skirt of Billy Travilla's ivory halter dress billows skyward. Though this was a common style of cocktail wear in the 1950s, it took Travilla – and his stunning star – to turn it into a showstopper. The plunging neckline ends in a tight band that wraps around Monroe's body, accented by an unexpectedly sweet bow belt that falls gently to the mid-calf skirt.

Travilla later said he was inspired by classical Greek sculpture, imagining Monroe as a modern-day goddess. And in 2011 the iconic costume became one of the most valuable outfits ever made, when it was bought at auction for $5.6 million.

There were thousands of New Yorkers crowding the set the day this image was shot, and Wilder had trouble controlling the scene. Unfortunately, one of the onlookers was Monroe's husband, Joe DiMaggio, who was outraged at the idea of so many strangers gawking at his wife's exposed undies. It was too much for an old-fashioned man who already resented her work, and the couple separated three weeks later.

1955

At Home with Arthur Miller

PHOTOGRAPHED BY SAM SHAW

By the time Monroe posed casually for Sam Shaw at the Long Island summer cottage she shared with her third husband, playwright Arthur Miller, she trusted him completely. She and Shaw had met several years earlier, when she was still an underappreciated contract player. In 1955, he took one of the most iconic photos of her career: the swirling-skirt image that was used to promote *The Seven Year Itch*.

Professionally, Monroe was firmly established by 1957. Personally, she was on shakier ground. Her marriage to Miller was already showing signs of strain, and she struggled with profound insecurities. Shaw allowed her to unwind – a rare luxury for a superstar who couldn't leave the house without full hair and makeup.

This period marked a deliberate retreat from Hollywood. Monroe had grown increasingly frustrated with an industry that was focused almost entirely on her looks. She spent much of her time on the East Coast, living in Connecticut and New York with Miller while studying at the Actors Studio.

In Shaw's photographs, she wears a cornflower blue sundress patterned with delicate white polka dots and piping – nothing flashy, just a simple cotton design with a gathered bust and a full, tiered skirt that skims her figure and moves easily in the breeze. With her natural hair and makeup, accessorized only by pretty flowers, Monroe looks more like the thoughtful young woman she believed herself to be than the bombshell the world insisted she was. The effect is tender, unguarded, and quietly revealing.

1957

Some Like It Hot

DIRECTED BY BILLY WILDER

By 1959, Monroe was one of the biggest stars in the world – and one of the most fragile. The pressures of fame had become almost unbearable and her insecurities were cresting. But she still longed to do great work, and Billy Wilder believed she could deliver. "She knew where the laugh was," he said, and cast her in *Some Like It Hot* as Sugar Kane, the singer and ukulele player in an all-female band called Sweet Sue and Her Society Syncopators.

Any Monroe appearance was an event, and famed Hollywood costume designer Orry-Kelly made the most of this one. A maestro of fabric and form, Orry-Kelly won his third Academy Award for the film's exquisite black-and-white wardrobe.

For Sugar's first appearance, he created a black satin dress that clung to his star while also catching the light. The jet-beaded fringe further highlighted her assets, drawing all eyes to her legs while turning Sugar into what Orry-Kelly called "a human shimmy."

The effect is both playful and sensual. As her bandmates fade into the background, Monroe stands out as though she's ethereally spotlit. Her platinum hair and pale skin glow against the monochrome palette, and the sophisticated glamour of her fur-trimmed traveling coat and feathered cloche make it clear that – as always – men will underestimate her only at their own risk.

1959

The Misfits

DIRECTED BY JOHN HUSTON

"Honey, when you smile it's like the sun coming up," the cowboy says to Monroe's stripper, Roslyn. We know just what he means.

Offscreen, Monroe was troubled. Her marriage to Miller, who had written *The Misfits* as a tribute to her, was coming undone, and she was struggling with the substance use that would eventually overcome her efforts to establish some stability. But onscreen, she is absolutely dazzling, and delivers the most complex and truthful work of her entire career. In lesser hands, Roslyn might have been just another stripper with a heart of gold, but Monroe plays her with wrenching delicacy, as a bruised and hesitant woman searching for kindness in a cold world.

After a quickie Reno divorce, Roslyn impulsively heads into the Nevada desert with Clark Gable's cowboy, Gay. Her emotional metamorphosis is reflected in her wardrobe, which Monroe personally oversaw. Within days, Roslyn has traded her chic black dresses for weathered Lady Levi's, and topped her simple white button-down shirts with a Lee's Storm Rider denim jacket (starting a trend we'd see later when stars like Paul Newman, Robert Redford, and Heath Ledger would wear the same blanket-lined style onscreen). She finishes off the transformation with dusty leather cowboy boots, from legendary western wear brand Hyer. Her carefully applied makeup is replaced too, with a fresh face and windblown hair. The simplicity suits her: She's finally dressing, and living, with ease and authenticity. Her only accessory is a thousand-watt smile that lights up the screen.

At this point in her career, Monroe's public image was so exaggerated it was almost cartoonish. But her performance in *The Misfits* is built on a wellspring of compassion. In Roslyn, she had the chance – however briefly – to reveal the Marilyn behind the myth.

1961

Happy Birthday, Mr. President

MADISON SQUARE GARDEN

When Monroe was invited to appear at President John F. Kennedy's 45th birthday celebration, she asked renowned costume designer Jean Louis for "a dress only Marilyn Monroe could wear." It's safe to say he delivered.

The night of the event, she stepped on stage wrapped in a sumptuous white ermine stole. The entire crowd gasped when she let it fall, revealing what would become one of the most famous frocks ever made.

Jean Louis had designed an early, and extraordinarily daring, version of the nude illusion gown – many of the offical sketches for this dress were drawn by Jean Louis's apprentice, Bob Mackie! This whisper of champagne soufflé silk, adorned with 2,500 crystals, was so tight it had to be stitched onto the star's body. Standing under the bright stage lights, Marilyn embodied the fantasy so many people believed her to be: shimmering, sexual, and (apparently) undressed.

The birthday serenade, sung in her most breathless and sultry fashion, drew another wave of astonishment. The only person in the room who appeared entirely unfazed – indeed, he was openly amused – was Kennedy himself. Their rapport has fueled decades of speculation, but whatever the truth may be, the lore of a secret romance took hold that night.

Sixty years later, Kim Kardashian borrowed the original gown and wore it to the Met Gala. But her homage simply underscored what the world already knew: There will only ever be one Marilyn Monroe.

1962

The Last Photos

PHOTOGRAPHED BY GEORGE BARRIS

When Marilyn sat for photographer George Barris in the summer of 1962, she was navigating one of the most difficult periods of her life. She felt misunderstood and undervalued in her career, and was exhausted by months of illness, personal conflict, and relentless public scrutiny. Rumors swirled around her – some grounded in truth, others in fantasy – and she carried the weight of them all. She had also just done a semi-nude shoot for *Vogue* with photographer Bert Stern, which had left her feeling exposed and exploited.

With Barris, a long-time friend, she finally had the opportunity to exhale. Their plan was to collaborate on a book, and Marilyn approached his camera with a rare openness. She arrived in her own clothes, many of them by Emilio Pucci, whose swirling patterns and bright monochromes she favored in the early 1960s. Her orange boatneck top and matching cigarette pants are strikingly simple. Her hair and makeup were equally minimal, in a quiet but clear rebuttal to the high-gloss aesthetic her fans expected.

Monroe was most comfortable when she could be casual, and for this shoot she wore a cable-knit cardigan as a robe on the Santa Monica beach. She allowed a hint of sexiness by going bare-legged, but she also clutched the sweater tight: She needed the protection of extra armor at this precarious moment in her life.

In allowing her to take the lead – something few men offered – Barris gave her the freedom, one last time, to share something of her inner self with the world.

1962

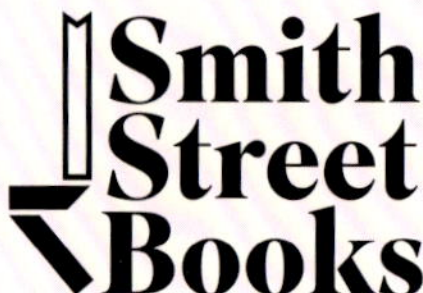

Published in 2026 by Smith Street Books
Naarm (Melbourne) | Australia
smithstreetbooks.com

Distributed outside of ANZ, North & Latin America by
Thames & Hudson Ltd., 6–24 Britannia Street, London, WC1X 9JD
thamesandhudson.com

EU Authorised Representative: Interart S.A.R.L.
19 rue Charles Auray, 93500 Pantin, Paris, France
productsafety@thameshudson.co.uk; www.interart.fr

ISBN: 978-1-9235-0325-0

Smith Street Books respectfully acknowledges the Wurundjeri People of the Kulin Nation, who are the Traditional Owners of the land on which we work, and we pay our respects to their Elders past and present.

Publisher: Hannah Koelmeyer
Project editor: Lucy Grant
Text: Elizabeth Weitzman
Text editor: Lorna Hendry
Illustrator: Kelly Smith
Design & layout: Susan Le
Production manager: Aisling Coughlan

Printed & bound in China by C&C Offset Printing Co., Ltd.

Book 457
10 9 8 7 6 5 4 3 2 1